some Posttribulationists Say the Darndest Things!
(About PreTrib Rapturists)

Fred DeRuvo

www.studygrowknow.com

Copyright © 2009 by Study-Grow-Know

All rights reserved. Written permission must be secured from the publisher to use or reproduce any part of this book, except brief quotations in critical reviews or articles.

Published in Scotts Valley, California, by Study-Grow-Know
www.studygrowknow.com • www.rightly-dividing.com

Scripture quotations are from The Holy Bible, English Standard Version®, copyright © 2001 by Crossway Bibles, a publishing ministry of Good News Publishers. Used by permission. All rights reserved.

Images used in this publication (unless otherwise noted) were created by the author, and are from clipartconnection.com and used with permission, ©2007 JUPITERIMAGES, and its licensors. All rights reserved.

Some original cartoons/images were created with ToonDoo, with copyright retained by Fred DeRuvo. For more information: http://www.toondoo.com/

All Woodcuts used herein are in the Public Domain and free of copyright.

All Figure illustrations used in this book were created by the author and protected under copyright laws, © 2009.

Cover design by Fred DeRuvo

Library of Congress Cataloging-in-Publication Data

DeRuvo, Fred, 1957 –

ISBN 0977424456
EAN-13 9780977424450

1. Religion – Christian Theology - Eschatology

Contents

Foreword:		5
Chapter 1:	Extra-Biblical	7
Chapter 2:	Deluded and Deceived	20
Chapter 3:	Gloom and Doom Prophets	26
Chapter 4:	Sarcasm Is As Sarcasm Does	34
Chapter 5:	Revisionism Revisited	44
Chapter 6:	With Vim and Vigor	53
Chapter 7:	Always Ready and Waiting?	58

This book is dedicated to my sister, Debbie,

who went home to be with her Lord and Savior on

November 2, 2008. Seems like it has been

forever, yet at times, it feels like it was

just yesterday that I stood by her as she

lay in a coma, in the hospital. She is

indeed free of her pain, and all that ailed her.

I look forward to seeing her again,

and enjoying eternity with her and all the saints.

FOREWORD

If you take the time to read what many Posttribulationists say about the PreTrib Rapture position (this normally extends to the person holding that position as well), it becomes quickly apparent that there is no love for the PreTrib Rapture or the individual holding that viewpoint. Sadly, we are often viewed as deluded and deceived. While this by itself might prompt feelings of sadness, they seem to quickly dissipate as this thought gives way to the assertion that because PreTrib Rapturists espouse a position that the Posttribbers sees as being against Scripture, the PreTrib Rapturist becomes the bad guy and the enemy of the cross.

The Pretribulation Rapture position is one in which all manner of accusations are made against it; many of them completely extra-biblical in nature, as if these hold at least as much weight (if not more), than any arguments taken directly from the Bible. The truth of the matter seems clear that people love to harp on what is considered to be the woeful inadequacy of the PreTrib Rapture position.

However, just what does all of this mean? When it comes right down to it, due to the original declaration and continued repetition over time of certain ideas, sentiments and statements, the PreTrib Rapture has come to be seen as not simply a doctrine that may not measure up to the truth of God's Word, but is much more than that. The PreTrib Rapture position has become a lightning rod of hatred, ignominy, and a great source of ridicule by those opposed to it.

In plain language, contempt for the PreTrib Rapture and the individual believing and espousing this doctrine is barely kept under wraps at best, and at worst, the gates of hell are brought to prevail against it. This form of contempt by the opposition is, in reality, nothing more than a sincerely blatant form of arrogance. Those holding to this position believe with all their heart, they are fighting the good fight, as they uphold God's standard. The problem though is that this lone position is seen as born of deception, while the other forms of the Rapture position might be viewed as wrong, but are not caricatured as being born in hell.

Though I previously published the book, *Does Believing and Espousing a PreTrib Rapture Create Unprepared Christians Doomed to Hell?,* I felt that this particular subject deserved something a bit less serious; something even somewhat tongue-in-cheek in its presentation. My efforts have resulted in this book, *(Some) Posttribulationists Say the Darndest Things (About PreTrib Rapturists).*

In truth, it is a bit humorous to hear all the reasons why the PreTrib Rapture position is thought to be wrong. Many of these reasons having nothing at all to do with Scripture. In this somewhat light-hearted look at these reasons, I would like to ask the reader for their patience and forgiveness if my approach to this subject offends them. That is really not my intent. My intent has more to do with seeing the reality of the meaning behind the claims and charges against the PreTrib Rapture position. I hope you enjoy this book...at least as much as I enjoyed writing it.

Fred DeRuvo, November 2009

Chapter 1
Extra-Biblical

To hear the Posttribber tell it, Dave MacPherson has proven his case lock, stock and barrel. It is airtight. He has apparently left no stone unturned and his journalistic integrity is clearly intact. All this stems from the eight books he has written on what he firmly believes is the Rapture cover-up, endearing him to those who oppose the PreTrib Rapture position.

Often, during discussions of the Rapture doctrine, arguments are presented from this source or that one, with many of these arguments emanating from an extra-biblical source. One individual said in an email to me, "*In numerous debates, I have attempted—sadly, to no avail—to get pretribulation rapturists to simply consider the Scriptures. Without fail, in each of these encounters Dispensationalists refer to extra-biblical material, misinterpret the Scriptures, and misunderstand what I am saying.*"[1]

Of course, the reality in comments noted above have more to do with his point of view and rhetoric, than in actual fact. His accusations regarding the alleged fact that PreTrib Rapturists do not "consider the Scriptures," (implying that we are constantly foisting extra-biblical

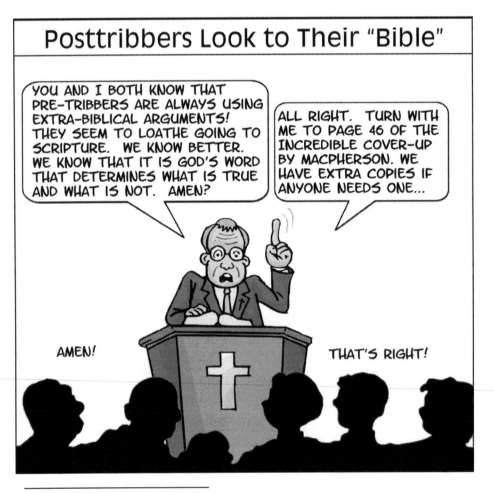

[1] Email on file from C. H. Fisher, 07/08/2009, 5:07p.m.

comments and argument on the Posttribber), are in actuality, completely off the mark. We will see why shortly.

In the early 1970s, MacPherson (himself a Posttribulationist as was his father before him), set about to find the "real" story behind the PreTrib Rapture origin, which had apparently been conveniently hidden from the light of day. Convinced that it was a relatively recent development, he believed the PreTrib Rapture origin must be a tale worth discovering and then telling. What he "found" was a cover-up that makes 9/11 looks like child's play. According to Mac, a young gal by the name of Margaret McDonald had a vision, in which she allegedly saw a PreTrib Rapture of the saints taking place before the seven year Tribulation period.

Taking his cue from McDonald, J. N. Darby, also allegedly heard of her vision and promptly decided that it was just what he needed to fill in the blanks, so to speak, of his theology. He began writing about this Rapture event, incorporating it into his own study notes. Later, another man (with dubious credentials, apparently), by the name Cyrus I. Scofield, happened along and liked what Darby had created. He then, began incorporating Darby's work into his own work. This work eventually became the Scofield Study System Bible, which he used in Bible studies that he led. The first version of the Scofield Study System Bible was published in 1909, and things took off from there.

It was at this point where, according to Mac, things began to take on the look of a covert operation. According to the beliefs of most folks who espouse the Posttrib Rapture position, the evangelical world at the time of Darby and Scofield was essentially Posttrib Rapture in position, but Darby, then Scofield managed to turn the tide. They managed this by flimflamming the entirety of the evangelical world, so that what *was* the alleged major belief was shoved to the side, replaced by the PreTrib Rapture position.

This story has been repeated many times, with many versions. Any Posttribber worth his salt, cannot get through a discussion of the Rapture without a nod to his guru, Dave MacPherson. Mac's writings are complete with casting aspersions on those within the PreTrib Rapture camp (referring to Dr. Thomas Ice, for instance, as one of the most "rabid" defenders of the PreTrib Rapture position). Yet, it is with certainty that the same title should be applied to MacPherson himself, since it is MacPherson who has taken on the whole of evangelicalism with his conveniently-created theory of the PreTrib Rapture origin.

MacPherson took it upon himself to attempt to overthrow single-handedly what he considers to be an error so humongous that it must have come from hell itself, in order to gain the notoriety it has gained. While it is very easy to accuse and to malign, the real difficulty is in the *proving*. Mac and his supporters believe unequivocally that he has left the PreTrib Rapturist with no recourse, but to concede defeat.

Dave MacPherson became a one-man crusade against what he considers to be an incorrect and therefore, unbiblical doctrine. Over time, others have come out of the woodwork, jumped onto his bandwagon and, as one might guess, their opinion mirrors MacPherson's in their support of this notion that the PreTrib Rapture position is a false one. Since much of MacPherson's reasoning rests in the severely convoluted testimony of a 15 year-old girl from the Victorian era, it becomes obvious that the one who is going outside of the Bible most often for arguments, is MacPherson himself. Since it becomes equally clear that Mac has never really proven anything with respect to Margaret McDonald, the Irvingites, J. N. Darby, or C. I. Scofield, he is merely creating muddy water in which he seems to enjoy swimming, while pulling others in with him. In fact, if Darby or Scofield were alive today, either might have a good case for a libel suit against MacPherson's charges, so devoid are

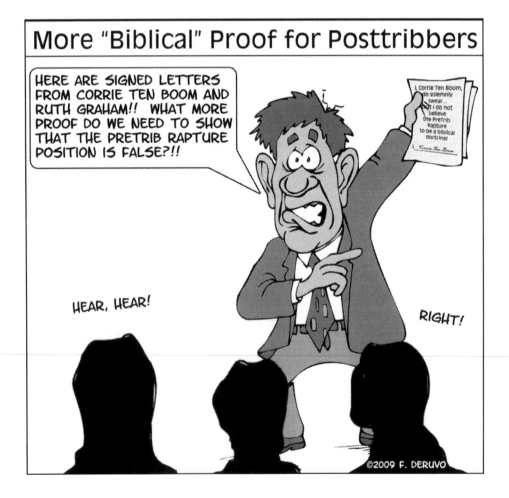

HOW TO BUILD A STRAWMAN ARGUMENT

1. TAKE STRAW
2. BUILD IN SHAPE OF MAN
3. KNOCK DOWN

A STRAWMAN ARGUMENT IS BUILT USING AN ERRANT, FLAWED OR IRRELEVANT ARGUMENT TO DIVERT ATTENTION FROM THE ORIGINAL ISSUE.

they of clear fact. The problem of course, is that it does not matter how many people *believe* the PreTrib Rapture to be false, or unbiblical. The only thing that matters is whether it *is actually* biblical or not, and this can *only* be determined by going to God's Word. As often as the Posttribulationist complains that Pretrib Rapturists supposedly ignore the Bible, preferring instead to rely on extra-biblical argumentation, in point of fact, the Posttribber is seen to do this just as often, more often defers to the extra-biblical argument more than the PreTribber does.

This is patently clear from Dave MacPherson's books alone, and since he is the "go-to" guy for the Posttribber, then it is not at all surprising that these Posttribbers use and rely on many of the same worn out, unproven strategies and reasons for rejecting the PreTrib Rapture position, as promulgated by MacPherson. None of MacPherson's books contain much in the way of biblical proof one way or the other that the PreTrib Rapture position is false. His opinion is uniformly reliant upon Margaret MacDonald and her alleged vision. That is the cover-up and there is the story, proof that the PreTrib Rapture doctrine is predicated upon the likes of a 15 year-old girl. When you start there, as far as Mac and his followers are concerned, what need is there for the Bible at all?

Though numerous "personalities" within Christendom have lined up in opposition against the PreTrib Rapture position, in essence, it does not matter. No amount of extra-biblical support or alleged documentation will *prove* or *disprove* something to be biblical. While these things can

offer something by way of potential circumstantial evidence, in the end, they turn out to be nothing more than that. Circumstantial evidence and opinion do not translate to biblical facts. All arguments – particularly those that are extra-biblical – need to be considered *against* Scripture.

The fact that Corrie Ten Boom, Ruth Graham, Dave MacPherson, or any other individual disagrees with the PreTrib Rapture and makes a statement against it, does not negate the doctrine itself. The fact that portions of the Pseudo-Ephraem document seem to favor the Posttrib Rapture scenario, while others appears to support the PreTrib Rapture ultimately means nothing. Though some argue for instance in another realm, that belief in the PreTrib Rapture fosters complacency and spiritual ineptitude, again, indicates nothing. This is merely a fabricated belief by some who suppose that espousers of the PreTrib Rapture become spiritually infantile. However, there is absolutely no proof of this at all. This is not only an extra-biblical argument, but an argument in which a straw man is created, and then easily eradicated. It can be said in response, that those who live with an imminent expectancy of His return, live with the proper attitude and demeanor, because as James tells us, those who look forward to one day seeing Him are purified (cf. 1 John 3:2-3).

In fact, it could just as easily be said that those who espouse the PreTrib Rapture are often far less angry and sarcastic than those who use energy and effort fighting against it. Just open any book by MacPherson, or those who have taken their cue from him. This would imply a potentially less than spiritually mature level on the part of the Posttribber and others who oppose the PreTrib Rapture, because of the carnal way in which they instigate and argue against the PreTrib Rapture position.

While many of these individuals may believe that they are right and the PreTrib Rapture position is not only wrong, but diabolically wrong, the way in which they enter the debate is questionable at best. It is common to read straw man arguments, judgmental words and phrases, which are used to tear down and eviscerate, rather than build up. These individuals are quick to judge, condemn and castigate, as they present their "case" against the PreTrib Rapture and the PreTrib Rapturist.

The PreTrib Rapturist is looked upon as one would look upon a Pharisee. Pharisees were legalists to the highest degree. They preferred the letter of the law, minus the spirit. Because they tended to object to just about everything that Jesus said and did, they represented whitewashed sepulchers, poisonous vipers, and worse. The attitude they possessed and brandished like a sword, was one that was dead set against God and His purposes. They were the blind leaders, who spouted a form of wisdom, yet without the power to change. These blind leaders led the average person of Israel, also blind *because* the Pharisees had no truth, and therefore, had nothing to give to the average Israelite, which would extricate them from their blindness. Jesus had the most condemnation for these leaders.

This is often how the PreTrib Rapturist is viewed; as someone who is deceived, and because they do not listen to the "truth" provided by the Posttribber, then they are also deluded, ultimately, resisting God. Because they deign to resist God, they are anathema; someone not to be pitied, but to be fully avoided. They would say that the PreTrib Rapturist's condemnation is deserved.

Once the PreTrib Rapturist resists all the alleged factual evidence presented to them by the Posttribber (along with everyone else who views the PreTrib Rapture position with disdain), the dust on each person's sandals should be shaken off in front of them. This will be a sure sign of their coming destruction. There is no love loss for the PreTribber, just as there is no love loss for the Christian Zionist by Anti-Zionists. In both cases, the PreTribber and Christian Zionist are seen as working *against* God. Since this is the case, and in both cases, (they are believed to be deceived), fully deceive multitudes with their anti-God beliefs, their coming judgment is deserved.

It is solely due to all the extra-biblical arguments that have been put forth that people have come to see the PreTribber as literally standing against God and His program. The PreTribber is deluded, deceived and teetering on the brink of destruction, because of the heretical origins of the PreTrib Rapture position. All other Rapture positions are somehow based on Scripture, but not the PreTrib Rapture position, which grew out of a diabolical event, and was merchandised by others.

We have moved far away from the Bible, and into the arena of public opinion. This public opinion (again, not based on Scripture, but on arguments proffered by those opposed to the PreTrib Rapture position), has created an atmosphere in which anger toward PreTribbers is justified. Since MacPherson's books have created a tone in which sarcasm is not only the accepted, but *expected* method of rebuttal, is it any wonder that there is a great deal of acrimony where the doctrine of the PreTrib Rapture is concerned?

What needs to happen is to get back to Scripture and remain there. Arguments based on a belief that MacPherson's books offer an unbiased, and therefore, a truthful view of actual history should be ignored since it is clear from the start that MacPherson merely has an axe to grind. Since the publication of his eight books against the PreTrib Rapture position (and with a plethora of books published in rebuttal and response), he has done nothing more than *preempt* actual biblically-based discussion, by whitewashing, revising and ignoring certain facts, while promoting others. A good deal of these facts play no part in determining the actual truth of either the origin, or biblical nature of the PreTrib Rapture doctrine.

One of the most loudly proclaimed arguments has to do with the "recent" origins of the PreTrib Rapture. It is assumed that all within the early church believed in a Posttrib Rapture position. This is based largely upon an argument from silence. Yet, if we look carefully at Paul's two letters to the Thessalonians, some important questions come to the fore, which stretch the imagination if Paul was supposedly a Posttrib Rapturist, as we are led to believe.

For instance, if Paul was *not* dealing with a PreTrib Rapture, why is there no discussion about the upcoming seven year Tribulation? Moreover, since it is clear from the letter itself that Paul had already taught the Thessalonians in person about these things, why on earth would the Thessalonians have been upset that those who had 'fallen asleep' might have missed 'that day?' If the subject was the Tribulation, there would have been no reason for the Thessalonians to be upset, but *happy* for those who had fallen asleep (died) before the Tribulation could begin!

Paul teaches them that the believers who had died had *not* missed it. Missed what? The day of the Lord. But then the question becomes just what exactly *is* the day of the Lord? Is it one particular day, or is it a period of time which may include the entirety of the Tribulation period, as well as the Rapture prior to it?

Paul tells them that the believers who fell asleep would be raised during that event, and they would be raised before those who were alive. Paul tells them not to be sad, as if they have no hope for those who have gone on ahead. The truth of the matter is that if the Tribulation was going to occur prior to the Rapture, with the Rapture happening at the very end of the Tribulation, then the fact that people had died before it began would be a cause for relief, not consternation.

These things and other arguments have taken a back seat because of the alleged conspiratorial beginnings of the PreTrib Rapture doctrine. No one discusses the Scriptural references any longer. Debate centers around MacPherson's books, which have shoved the Bible off to the side. Yet, the PreTrib Rapturist is the one who is accused of delving heavily into the extra-biblical area, in spite of the fact that had not one of MacPherson's books been written, there would be no need to respond to his accusations, most of which are soundly outside of Scripture.

Chapter 2
Deluded and Deceived

One of the overarching arguments against the veracity of the PreTrib Rapture position is the idea that those who believe and espouse it, do so because they are deceived and deluded. To date, absolutely no biblical evidence is presented for this argument, as a cause and effect, but that does not matter because it *sounds* convincing. It is very much like accusing someone of being a witch in the past. Though the claims and charges often rested on the "he said/she said" type of accusation, once the charge was leveled, the oneness was on the accused to disprove the charge.

Often, the argument goes something like this: because of the questionable origin of the PreTrib Rapture doctrine, and because of the number of people who have publicly stated that it is a doctrine not based on the Bible, its origin is therefore Satanic, and the people who agree with the doctrine are themselves, spiritually deceived.

This spiritual deception is cause for alarm. Those who do not ascribe to the PreTrib Rapture doctrine, believe it to be their calling in life to do whatever is necessary to extricate the PreTrib Rapturist from their beguiled position, since to many, this position connects to a person's salvation. Once they have done all they can to accomplish this to no avail, then the PreTrib Rapturist ceases to be the subject of rescue and becomes the *contributor to the ongoing problem*.

At this point, the PreTrib Rapturist is seen as the enemy of the cross; a heretic, justifiably condemned by others within Christendom, and ignored; treated as a leper. The "spiritual" Posttribulationist retreats from the leprous PreTrib Rapturist, convinced in the knowledge that "he tried" to save a deceived soul from perishing, but was unable to do so. Now, with the dust shaken from his feet, he resolves to move on, helping others whose lives are endangered by the overarching and tragic lie of the PreTrib Rapture.

It must be remembered that this charge (that the PreTrib Rapture stems solely from a conspiracy, which under the best of circumstances, has *not* been proven by Dave MacPherson, or anyone else, and at worst, is simply libelous), is what the Posttribulationist hangs his hat on. No Scripture references are issued, proving any type of conspiracy, or deception. This conspiratorial, extra-biblical argument stems solely from what people have *said* about the PreTrib Rapture. Having been stated enough times, it has become "fact" that to many, is simply irrefutable.

The brouhaha that has developed because of one man's campaign against a doctrine with which he does not agree seems much more of a conspiracy than the alleged conspiracy MacPherson is supposed to have unearthed! There is no more reason to claim that the PreTrib Rapture position is based on a devilish delusion than to believe that either the Mid-Trib, or Pre-Wrath Rapture positions are based on such.

Clearly, only one Rapture position can be correct (and for the time being, let us not include those who hold to a "no Rapture" position). If this is the case, then would it not stand to reason that *any* position other than the true position falls in the category of delusion, born of spiritual deception? However, as far as Posttribbers are concerned, this is not the case at all.

The only Rapture position in which people believe it to be ascended from the pit of hell is the PreTrib Rapture position. Why is this? Simply due to the reasons laid out on this book's cover and many others found within the writings of Dave MacPherson. If the PreTrib Rapturist is deceived into believing that they will be gone *prior* to the Tribulation - Great Tribulation period, then it obviously results in carnal living, a complete lack of spiritual maturity, and relative ease in living a lifestyle in which Self is on the throne, while Christ is relegated to the back storeroom (if considered at all). This is simply a case of people creating straw man arguments and then knocking them down. While the arguments themselves *seem* to have merit, when realistically considered, they fail miserably to verify the charges against them.

Consider the fact that there are only a *few* television evangelists who, with great pomp and circumstance, live a lifestyle effervescent with over the top carnality, yet attempt to pass themselves off as authentic Christians. It is not difficult to tune into a broadcast of a program purporting to be Christian in flavor, with the host or hostess, adorned in pompadours, the latest suits and gowns, and an entourage that fills their every whim and command as if spoken by God Himself. Because some of these individuals believe and espouse the idea of a PreTrib Rapture does not negate the soundness of the doctrine. These individuals are not the norm. They are decadently *abnormal and by no means represent biblical Christianity*. The fact that they delude their listeners into coughing up millions of dollars yearly has nothing to do with the veracity of a doctrine. They do not even care (or know), whether the individuals who support their "ministry" are Christians!

Many of these same television personalities also stress the deity of Christ, His virgin birth and resurrection as well as other orthodox views

within Christendom. Should we then alter our belief in these doctrines because the same people who have made a mockery of what it means to be an authentic Christian are espousing them?

The real problem is not in any doctrine itself, but the fact that some individuals like those above espouse them *and* profit from them. Yet, we do not attempt to uncover some underlying conspiracy surrounding the deity of Christ, just because these folks who teach and preach a PreTrib Rapture message, also believe in the deity of Christ.

There are many, *many* authentic Christians, who daily give of their lives – physically, emotionally and financially – to help others who are in *need*, but also believe in a PreTrib Rapture. These people no sooner sit back, relax and live a lifestyle of sinning because they somehow think that they need not worry about the future. While they may believe that when it really starts getting tough down here on this planet, Jesus will swoop down and rescue them, rapturing them into the heavens, they are also well-versed in daily trials and tribulations and do not shy away from them. They recognize that the testing of our faith produces perseverance and spiritual maturity in Christ. This is the only way it is produced within each Christian.

In truth, I do not know *one* PreTrib Rapturist who believes and therefore lives like a depraved sinner. We are committed to Christ, serve Him daily, suffer with Him and those who love Him when they have to deal with the loss of a loved one, or sickness, or other needs.

I have been a Christian since the age of 13, and have attended numerous churches. Now 52, I have never ever seen the level of commitment of Christians that is evidenced at the church I now attend and have been a member of for a number of years. This is a church largely full of PreTribbers. The level of love and service in witnessed by these saints of the Lord is astounding and encouraging.

Frankly, I have grown tired of the rancor tossed about because of the Posttribbers' verdict of me and other PreTribbers. It is unconscionable that while the lost of the world heads toward hell, the Posttribber looks aghast at the Pretribber and shakes his finger, with a holier than thou attitude. The coming apostasy is largely blamed on the PreTrib Rapture position, yet it is clear that the Posttribbers are unable to see past their own lack of spiritual adroitness.

This world is *already* in the midst of severe apostasy and none of it has anything to do with the PreTrib Rapture position. Recently, in a newsletter from *Understanding the Times*, Jan Markell neatly and succinctly summed up the problem within the visible church today:

- the mystical movement
- the emergent church
- seeker-sensitive church growth movement
- Churches going green
- ignoring the literality of the Bible
- kingdom now/dominion theology[2]

Not one of the things mentioned by Jan is predicated on the PreTrib Rapture position. The arrogance that emanates from the Posttrib people is without basis.

Here is a truth that must be recognized by all: our *deaths* may occur long before any Rapture *or* Tribulation. Are we ready? The False prophets are definitely at work in the church, but if you'll note the bulleted list above, there is far more going on that it seems Posttribbers can see.

---

[2] http://www.understandthetimes.org/

Chapter 3
Gloom and Doom Prophets

Time and time again, like the consistent dripping of a leaky faucet, we hear the pronouncement that the PreTrib Rapture position is born of deceit, resting on dubious origins. However, this same proclamation of deceitful origins does not apply to other Rapture positions. In fact, though the Posttribber may come out strongly against these other positions – Mid-Trib, Pre-Wrath, etc. – the word "deceived" is normally not heard in connection with them. This is reserved solely for those within the PreTrib Rapture camp. It is the PreTrib Rapture position, which is seen as the one causing the most harm, due to its controversial beginnings. This harm is created because apparently, it is believed that those who espouse a PreTrib Rapture doctrine, have literally stopped (or never actually began), living a godly life.

The reasoning is that since the PreTribber believes that he will be "caught up" before the time of the final Tribulation actually begins, then he has no need to worry. All Christians will be raptured to safety before things get thoroughly troublesome. Because this will occur, it follows that the PreTrib Rapturist has absolutely no reason to live a godly life. Because he has no reason to live a godly life, he does not. Does anyone see the arrogance in this position espoused by those opposed to the PreTrib Rapture position? Because Posttribbers believe that the PreTrib Rapture is wrong from the start (having gone *outside* the Bible to determine its origins), reasons are then *created* to support *why* it is wrong, seemingly from a biblical perspective. These particular reasons – though seeming to be spiritual, but in actuality, not biblically based – are put forth as examples to show what happens when people believe something that is said to *be un*true.

Those who fully believe every word that MacPherson and others have stated about the origins of the PreTrib Rapture, the results of adopting the PreTrib Rapture position become obvious and even self-fulfilling.

These individuals point to well-known people who believe and espouse a PreTrib Rapture position, such as Tim LaHaye, or Thomas Ice, or Grant Jeffrey, or others. They then point to the "wealth" of these individuals, especially LaHaye, and they believe that this, in and of itself, *proves* their point. In other words, far from being truly and spiritually mature in Christ, the implication (and sometimes, the actual stated comment), is that these individuals have promoted this false theory of the PreTrib Rapture, solely for financial gain.

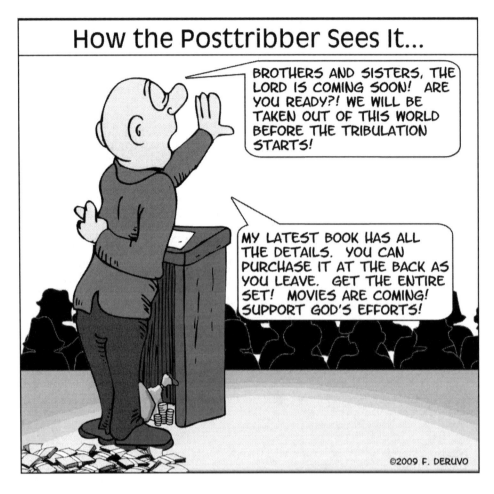

These individuals are often referred to as "Doom and Gloom Profiteers," or something similar, because fear tends to sell books and in the case of LaHaye, it sells movies as well. Apparently, LaHaye is exulting on piles and piles of money, knowing that the PreTrib Rapture doctrine is false from the start, but prefers to continue to push it because of the financial gain he receives from it. This type of thinking is wrong on any number of levels, not least of which is the severely judgmental attitude.

The PreTrib Rapture is viewed by some almost as if it was a pyramid scheme! The more people you can get underneath you who also believe and try to "sell" the theory, the more money the top person makes. The

truth of the matter is that aside from a few individuals who are seen as "celebs" of the PreTrib Rapture position, most individuals are simply hard-working, Jesus-loving, church-going, God-fearing, average Christians, who serve God by serving one another and witnessing to the lost of the world. If LaHaye's and Ice's books sell, wonderful.

There is no proof at all that individuals who believe the PreTrib Rapture doctrine do so because it somehow makes them rich, yet this is often repeated as if it is a fact. This is only nothing more than *opinion.* While there are any number of charlatans out there who preach many of the orthodox doctrines of the faith, purely for filthy lucre, this does not prove that everyone and anyone who sells books, receives remuneration for their speaking engagements, or makes movies *is* cut from the same cloth. While some do go into the ministry for the sake of profit, and to enrich themselves from their money-making scheme, not all are so moved.

Should we castigate and condemn all those individuals who have made money from any books they sell, whose career it is to go from place to place, speaking on the things of the Lord? Should we ostracize, criticize and reprimand all Christians, who write a book, assuming they are guilty of self-promotion, or using Christianity as a tool to gain riches? No one forces anyone to buy a book. No one insists that they must fork out $10 to see a movie. These are extras that people do not need, but often purchase for their growth.

My own library contains over 1,000 books and simply by looking at them, it would be impossible to determine what my theological position is on nearly any subject. I do not just buy those books from authors with whom I agree, ignoring others who might have something important to say.

There are many preachers – both televised and not – throughout this world whose views run the doctrinal gamut. Because we do not agree with them, or because we may view their positions as even heretical may not mean that they do what they do for the sake of money. They may do what they do because they really believe that they are able to help people, even though they are way off doctrinally speaking.

There are also any number of individuals who are well known who are so obviously conning their followers that the question becomes "how could their followers be so naïve?" However, as already mentioned, we do not throw out the deity of Christ, or the belief in the virgin birth because some television charlatan also uses it to widen their own earthly kingdom while increasing their net worth.

Apparently, though, from a Posttribbers' perspective, anyone who believes something strongly enough and writes a book about it, or makes a movie from it, is doing so for the *sole purpose* of making a ton of money…IF it has anything to do with the PreTrib Rapture. In LaHaye's case, he has written his share of books on personalities long before he ever began writing on the PreTrib Rapture. If he made his "wealth," he made it from that end of his career prior to moving into the area of Eschatology.

Surely, the same could be said about the individuals who write *against* the PreTrib Rapture. It must be stated that without Dave MacPherson's first (of eight books) on the subject, would there have been a real need to write as many books in rebuttal to his? One individual wrote to tell me that Dave MacPherson has never kept one penny of sales from any of his books; donating all of it to charities. Beyond this, I was informed that MacPherson drives a very old beater of a car and lives with his wife, operating a hotel in the southwestern United States. In other words, he lives a pauper's lifestyle.

The individual's actual quote, in response to one of my blogs, states *"How can you claim that MacPherson has 'been making money hand over fist'? He has stated that all of his book royalties have always gone to a nonprofit corporation and not to himself or any other individual. During the last 20 years he and his wife have lived at a motel in southeastern Utah that she helps to run. And their only vehicle is a 17-year-old Toyota. The ones who HAVE made money hand over fist are millionaire pretrib traffickers like Lindsey and LaHaye, both of whom live sumptously in Palm Springs, California!*[3]

Requested documentation from the individual, was never received, by way of follow-up. As of this writing, we are still attempting to track the truth of this information down. Frankly, if MacPherson actually lives like this, then more power to him, but if this is the case, it is confusing why this information would not be more readily available to the public.

---

[3] http://modres.wordpress.com/2009/09/17/the-pretrib-rapture-and-being-allegedly-unprepared/?preview=true&preview_id=215&preview_nonce=c2ca764ad0

The closest I came to it is finding other people who repeated the same information they apparently heard on a radio program either hosted by MacPherson, or where he was a guest. In either case, I would like to see it in written form by MacPherson. I would also be very much interested in knowing to which organization(s) MacPherson's royalties go. In other words, does MacPherson's money go to any organization of which he is connected to in any way, shape or form? If so, does he have access to that money once it reaches that organization? Hmmm, sounds like a job for an investigative journalist...with a great deal of integrity. Anyone? Anyone? Buehler?

It is also our understanding (after doing some research) that Mr. MacPherson is preparing for the Tribulation by living in an earthen home, in survivalist mode. That is interesting. It would be nice to know more of Dave's plans to be a witness during this period of time that will come upon the entire earth. Does he intend to hide during the entire seven years, or will he be out on the front lines, witnessing to the lost of this world? As time winds down, segueing into eternity, does Dave plan on becoming part of the army that has marching orders from the Lord to witness to the world, whether they listen or not? Inquiring minds want to know...

Chapter 4

Sarcasm is as Sarcasm Does

The comments are becoming more and interesting...and volatile. Aside from putting a huge question mark over the genuineness of the PreTrib Rapture position, Dave MacPherson has created groupies, which mirror his tone and ferocity. These followers pull no punches in their condemnation of the PreTrib Rapture doctrine and those who hold to it. Why do they do this? It is because Dave MacPherson does this. His attitude, demeanor, and expressed rancor provide permission for those who think like him, to do the same thing.

It is extremely easy for most people to be sarcastic. The phrase "Sarcasm: It's my second language" is all too familiar to most of us, and we understand it because of how easily we can fall into a diatribe-laced rebuttal, abounding with sarcastic comments. The *problem* with sarcasm is twofold:

1. Once it is out there, it is impossible to retract.
2. Moreover, *like* begets *like*.

In other words, when someone offers an opinion dripping with sarcasm, it is not long before the other individual does the same thing. What this can (and often does), lead to is an all out war of words, which serves absolutely no purpose at all, except to incite to greater degrees of anger and contempt.

Cruising the 'Net brings much of this into our homes via our computer monitors. There are a million and one comments out there from individuals who bristle at the very thought of the PreTrib Rapture doctrine. What they often fail to see is how ironic their comments truly are, although they believe their sarcasm so conveniently and obviously makes their points evident, and because of that, the sarcasm is excused as the accepted form of delivery.

By way of example, here is an interesting comment from someone who preferred not to use their real name, choosing simply to go by the name of "Anonymous" on one forum:

"Congratulations! You are now fulfilling the Bible which says "Come now, and let us repeat together." Be sure to repeat what Walvoord, Lindsey, LaHaye, Ice etc. repeat what their own teachers repeat what their own teachers repeat etc. etc. etc.! Repeat that Christ's return is imminent because we're told to "watch" (Matt. 24, 25) for it. So is the "day of God" (II Pet. 3:12) - which you admit is at least 1000 years ahead - also imminent because we're told to be "looking for" it? Also repeat the pretrib myths about the "Jewish wedding stages" and "Jewish feasts" (where's your "church/Israel dichotomy" now?) even though Christ and

Paul knew nothing about a "pretrib stage" and neither did any official theological creed or organized church before 1830!"[4]

The first thing we note is *sarcasm*. MacPherson would undoubtedly be proud, since he has fostered this approach in every book he has written concerning the PreTrib Rapture. What this particular poster fails to understand is that *he* is *dutifully repeating* what he has learned from Dave MacPherson and others. No one has an original thought in this debate. The same arguments and reasons are tossed from one side to the other.

The person notes (with ample sarcasm), that:

- Christ's "imminent" return could not possibly mean *at any time*
- References to the "Jewish wedding stages" and "Jewish feasts" are myths, or forced logic

---

[4] https://www.blogger.com/comment.g?blogID=8276258682872785611&postID=1463229237414310308&page=1&isPopup=true

- He declaratively states that neither Christ or Paul knew nothing of a PreTrib Rapture stage, nor did the official creeds before 1830

All of the above is simply *reiterating* what Dave MacPherson and other writers and researchers have stated regarding the PreTrib Rapture position. However, the person who made the post has the temerity to accuse another individual of merely repeating things that Walvoord, and others have stated. Does he not see the irony in his own words, since he is merely parroting MacPherson? If he *does* see this, to him, it is likely acceptable in his case, because MacPherson is viewed as someone who has brought "truth" back into the arena where it was apparently completely absent prior.

The other thing that is immediately noted is the misconception of the meaning of "imminency." Some Posttribbers go out of their way to argue that the concept of imminency is something that was altogether unknown by Jesus or the apostles. This is because many Posttribbers apply a different meaning to the word, understand "imminent" to mean "soon." However, the word actually means, *"could happen at any moment."* This is exactly what Paul, Peter, Jesus and others mean when they speak of His coming for His Bride as something that is *imminent*. It could happen at any moment and a number of parables bear this out.

The belief that the stages of the Jewish wedding are a myth is a commonly mistaken position, espoused by those opposed to the PreTrib Rapture position. In fact, a number of authors support the reality of the stages of the Jewish wedding. John Klein and Adam Spears detail this quite well in their book *Volume 1 Lost in Translation Series: Rediscovering the Hebrew Roots of Our Faith*. Beginning on page 53, they discuss the Ancient Hebrew Betrothal period. They explain, *"…marriage is the culmination of the three previous types of covenant: servanthood, friendship, and inheritance. That explains why the*

Stages of Jewish Marriage and the Church

Stage 1 - Father of Groom Arranges Marriage/Pays Bride Price

Husbands, love your wives just as Christ loved the church and gave himself for her to sanctify her by cleansing her with the washing of the water by the word, so that he may present the church to himself as glorious – not having a stain or wrinkle, or any such blemish, but holy and blameless. Ephesians 5:25-27

Stage 2 - Groom Fetches the Bride (Rapture)

For we tell you this by the word of the Lord, that we who are alive, who are left until the coming of the Lord, will surely not go ahead of those who have fallen asleep. For the Lord himself will come down from heaven with a shout of command, with the voice of the archangel, and with the trumpet of God, and the dead in Christ will rise first. Then we who are alive, who are left, will be suddenly caught up together with them in the clouds to meet the Lord in the air. And so we will always be with the Lord. Therefore encourage one another with these words. 1 Thessalonians 4:15-18

Stage 3 - Wedding Ceremony with Church (Bride)

Then I heard what sounded like the voice of a vast throng, like the roar of many waters and like loud crashes of thunder. They were shouting: "Hallelujah! For the Lord our God, the All-Powerful, reigns! Let us rejoice and exult and give him glory, because the wedding celebration of the Lamb has come, and his bride has made herself ready. She was permitted to be dressed in bright, clean, fine linen" (for the fine linen is the righteous deeds of the saints). Revelation 19:6-8

Stage 4 - Marriage Feast

The wedding is ready, but the ones who had been invited were not worthy. So go into the main streets and invite everyone you find to the wedding banquet. Matthew 22:8-9

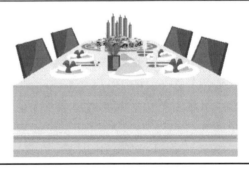

©2009 F. DERUVO

marriage relationship is so central to everything God ordained. In scripture after scripture, God identifies Himself as the Bridegroom, and He compares all those who enter into all three forms of covenant with Him as the bride. His own references to that fundamental image fill the Old Testament, from the stories of the patriarchs to the words He put in the mouths of the prophets."[5]

The authors then discuss the steps involved in the ancient Hebrew marriage tradition, which included[6] (information below is paraphrased):

- A tentative match mutually identified by parents
- Eventually, the prospective bridegroom brought the father to the bride's home. They carried the betrothal cup, wine and anticipated bride price in a pouch. They arrived and knocked.
- The prospective bride's father would be on the other side of the door. He would peek out to see who was there. He would identify the visitors, and then look to this daughter for confirmation.
- Should he open the door? If "yes" a fully functional marriage was made at that point. Once the door was open and visitors were invited in, and the actual marriage agreement was worked out. This step parallels *salvation*.
- If the bride said "no," the groom and father would make a u-turn and head for home. The bride was the only one who could back out at this point and she needed no reason at all.
- There were four cups of wine during this process. Once inside, the father and groom worked out the details, during dinner with her family.

---

[5] John Klein and Adam Spears, *Volume 1 Lost in Translation Series: Rediscovering the Hebrew Roots of Our Faith* (Tennessee: Selah Publishing Group 2007), 53
[6] Ibid, 54-74

- Cup Number One: (Sanctification) Drank this cup once inside the home. The bride and groom are setting one another apart for the other.
- Cup Number Two: (also called Cup of Betrothal, Cup of Plagues, Cup of Bargaining, or Cup of Dedication) Only bride, groom and two fathers drink this, representing the covenant between the two families to become eternal friends. This corresponds with the *ketubah.* The details of the marriage worked out – how would groom support bride? What skills did groom possess? Was the wife a Proverbs 31 wife? Jesus often referred to Himself as the Bridegroom.
- Cup Number Three: (Cup of Redemption, or Cup of Inheritance) Signified shared inheritance of the marriage partners. The bride and groom only consumed this cup at the end of the meal. This also officially sealed the marriage agreement between them. Following this, the young men of the family would hit the streets blowing their ram's horns (shofars), announcing to everyone that a marriage contract had been signed. After third cup has been consumed, three things need to be accomplished:
    - Groom had to pay bride price (30 pieces of silver)
    - Groom must go and prepare a place for his bride
        - Groom remained under ironclad rule of his father. His father decided *when* the preparations were sufficient and complete, just as Jesus did not know the day or hour (cf. Mark 13:32).
    - The bridesmaids' job was to watch for the groom's arrival. When they saw him coming, their lamps would show the way. They were also expected to warn the bride (cf. Matthew 25:1-13).

- Cup Number Four: (Cup of Praise) Shared between the bride and groom only during the actual wedding ceremony. For the Christian, they share this cup on the day of the wedding with Christ.

The authors also explain what a *ketubah* is and how it applies to the Christian. Essentially, it is a marriage contract and a completed document has five parts to it[7]:

1. A combined family history of bride and groom
2. Personal family history of the bride
3. Personal family history of the groom
4. The story of how the bride and groom met
5. Detailed listing of both bride's and groom's responsibilities before and after the wedding

According to Klein and Spears, these five aspects relate to the first five books of the Bible, also known as the Torah:

1. Genesis – combined family history of bride and groom
2. Exodus – personal and family history of bride
3. Leviticus – history of God's "family," the Levites
4. Numbers – God's love affair with His people; joys and sorrows as He reaches out to His bride
5. Deuteronomy – specifies responsibilities of both bride and groom

The *mikveh,* according to the authors occurs *"A few hours before dawn, the groom and his men would leave the bride with her bridesmaids. Her friends would lead her to the* mikveh, *a ceremonial bath where she would be bathed in running ('living') water. As in every Hebrew mikveh, or baptism, she would bow forward into the oncoming stream, facing the*

---

[7] John Klein and Adam Spears, *Volume 1 Lost in Translation Series: Rediscovering the Hebrew Roots of Our Faith* (Tennessee: Selah Publishing Group 2007), 66

source as an act of love and submission to God, the source of all life...following the mikveh, the bride's attendants would anoint her with fragrant oils, and she would return home to rest for a few hours before the morning."[8]

There are numerous references from other Jewish believers who understand the Jewish wedding process, seeing it as symbolically played out in the redemption of the Church; Christ's Bride. Of course, Posttribbers and others have no difficulty in finding one or two Jewish rabbis who disagree that the Jewish marriage process actually existed at all. That is to be expected. It is no different from one author, who was able to locate two historians who believed not that World War I was the actual First World War, but that the War of Spanish Succession actually has that title. So that particular author, in attempting to negate the beliefs that Jesus' words "nation against nation, and kingdom against kingdom," in the Olivet Discourse refers to a global conflict which nearly

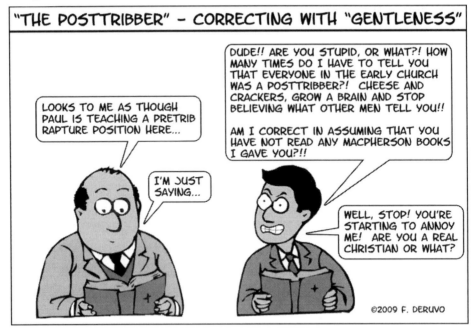

---

[8] John Klein and Adam Spears, *Volume 1 Lost in Translation Series: Rediscovering the Hebrew Roots of Our Faith* (Tennessee: Selah Publishing Group 2007), 69-70

100% of historians and people in general attribute to World War I, found two historians (now deceased) who disagreed with that conception. The truth seems to be obvious though, in spite of one man deigning to rewrite and revise historical meaning.

There was a Jewish wedding process and we see it throughout Scripture. God uses the terminology of the wedding process repeatedly, to refer symbolically to Christ's union with His bride. It would appear that the PreTrib Rapture position has merit in seeing the stages of the wedding process involved in the full redemption of the Church, which includes the Rapture of the Church *prior* to the Tribulation.

Chapter 5
Revisionism Revisited

The charges and claims continue unabated. To hear the Posttribulationist tell it, not only is the PreTrib Rapture fabricated completely, with its beginning after the 1830s, but those who believe the PreTrib Rapture doctrine to be true, are guilty of revising history and through their documentation of it.

Some individuals are so quick to grab hold of this charge and run with it, that they do not even consider the fact that MacPherson himself may be guilty of the same thing. Certainly, if any from the PreTrib Rapture camp attempted to foist this same charge on MacPherson or any of his works, there would be an outcry of epic proportions! Posttribbers and others would not stand for this insult; that MacPherson – a self-proclaimed investigative journalist – could be guilty of contriving evidentiary information on his own behalf, in order to make the facts look as though they supported his efforts. This would be incomprehensible. It simply could *not* happen (...*snort*!)!

After reading MacPherson's The Rapture Plot, Frank Marotta reviewed the book and wrapped up his review with these words, "*Dave MacPherson's The Rapture Plot is a defective work which distorts history. There is no plot. It misrepresents godly men such as Darby and Kelly. It fails to prove the Irvingites were pretribulational in the 1830s. It is completely inaccurate concerning Morgan Edwards' teaching. The Rapture Plot has the same character as MacPherson's previous works. Christians who desire to feed their souls on truth would be well advised to avoid his works.*"[9]

However, someone might come along and simply accuse Marotta of being an angry PreTribber attempting to get back at MacPherson by hauling his work over the coals. Maybe, but if so, then he certainly spends plenty of time researching MacPherson's claims, responding to many of them, point by point.

Marotta points out that in all of his own research, he has "*never found a claim that anyone outside their group 'stole' their doctrines*" (referring to the Catholic Apostolic and Irvingite works). Marotta then points to historian William Bramley-Moore, who specialized in the Catholic Apostolic movement and, notes Marotta, was "*a contemporary of William Kelly.*"[10]

---

[9] http://www.according2prophecy.org/macphers.html
[10] Ibid

Marotta seems to blow a huge hole in MacPherson's contrived position, simply by referencing Bramley-Moore. He states, "*In his work The Church's Forgotten Hope, (a significant work never discussed by MacPherson) Bramley-Moore skips over Margaret Macdonald and credits John Asgill in 1703 as '. . . the only individual who, since the Reformation [until 1830] had given a clarion testimony' to the hope of translation (p. 251)! We will not manufacture a 'plot' or 'cover-up' regarding the failure of MacPherson and others to credit Asgill. (Asgill taught that individual translation was possible, similar to Enoch or Elijah. His view is distinct from pretribulationism.) More relevant to our discussion, Bramley-Moore never claimed the brethren or anyone else*

'stole' the Irvingite prophetical views."[11]

Interesting, is it not? In truth, this has not come as a shock to this author, who has himself noticed MacPherson's penchant for revising documentation and history to suit his own purposes. This is clear when reading MacPherson's views on the Pseudo-Ephraem document.

Like anything else, there are *many* opinions as to what the Pseudo-Ephraem document means. What it ALL boils down to is what people want to see in that particular document. MacPherson defers to Dr. Paul Alexander, who believes the phrase "gathered to the Lord" references a Catholic doctrine referring only to acts on earth, and not being raptured off earth at all. In Alexander's opinion then, the comments made by the writer of the Pseudo-Ephraem document are supposedly of Catholic origin, when in point of fact, if the document is as old as experts believe it may be, Catholicism would have *barely* begun.

Why are we not able to take the document's words as they are? If we do, the obvious meaning of "gathered to the Lord" negates the Posttribulation position, within the Pseudo-Ephraem document. If the phrase is correctly understood as written, then the only thing Posttribulationalists can say is something along the lines of, "*Gee, there's only **one** document out there that supports the PreTrib Rapture position?*" as some have already stated.

The point remains – that MacPherson completely glossed over the part in Section 2, where people are gathered to the Lord *before* the Tribulation. He at first seems to pretend as if the phrase does not exist within the document. While there is debate about its meaning for some, the obvious meaning is clear. Dr. Alexander's opinion on the matter is no more final than anyone else's. The reality is that *each* person *decides*

---

[11] http://www.according2prophecy.org/macphers.html

what he or she will, or will not believe about something. This is based on a predilection for a certain and specific theory about the PreTrib Rapture. It is that simple.

MacPherson himself has an axe to grind because he grew up in a household in which Posttribulationalism was the normal belief. It is because of that position that he opposes the PreTrib Rapture position. The reason why MacPherson glosses over some pertinent facts, while ignoring others seems fairly obvious.

Why is it that people like MacPherson are so adept at callously dealing with people they do not agree with, yet when reading Ice, Jeffrey, Ryrie, Walvoord, or others, there is no sense that they *hate* the person with which they disagree? MacPherson's arrogance precedes him and it will be his downfall. There is nothing God-honoring in his rhetoric. Nothing.

THE NEXT IN THE LINE OF "CONSPIRACIES"

THE NEXT "BESTSELLER" BY A FAMOUS AUTHOR! ABLE TO GO WHERE NO OTHER COUNTRY OR GOVERNMENT HAS GONE!

AN INTERVIEW WITH BIN LADEN THAT WILL ROCK YOUR WORLD!

FIND OUT WHY AND HOW THIS MAN IS NOTHING MORE THAN A PUPPET WHOSE I.Q. BARELY TIPS THE SCALES AT 50, HAS BEEN AT THE CENTER OF THE WORLD'S ATTENTION, YET ONLY YEARNS TO HELP THE POOR, FEED THE HUNGRY AND DO WHAT IS RIGHT!

FIND OUT WHY HE IS SO HATED; WHY HE IS SO MALIGNED WE GO DEEP INTO THE UNDERGROUND LAIR OF THE MOST WANTED MAN IN THE WORLD!

©2009 F. DERUVO

Many books and articles exist documenting all the places where MacPherson went wrong. To his followers though, he is *not* wrong. In fact, there are any number of published books and articles, in which MacPherson is once again, portrayed as the hero to those pitted against the PreTrib Rapture position. These individuals have come out against Marotta, and others. Robert Gundry has allegedly dismantled the Pseudo-Ephraem document, piece by piece, showing once and for all, that it is a Posttrib document. Ultimately, though, like all opinions, they are only as factual as the people who believe them.

Those who refuse to acknowledge MacPherson has allegedly uncovered the truth about the PreTrib Rapture origins are said to be simply attacking him. It does not matter to MacPherson's followers that he seems to be a master reviser himself, or that he uses a bit of sleight of hand to ignore certain aspects of history to achieve his ends. What matters to his followers is they have real reasons to believe that the

PreTrib Rapture doctrine is false, and those reasons all lie in the 'fact' of an alleged cover-up.

People love a good conspiracy theory. MacPherson has certainly created what would appear to be a masterful cover-up, perpetrated by a few individuals, who managed to "sell" their artificial doctrine of the PreTrib Rapture to the entirety of the evangelical world. That, in and of itself, is enough to make red flags go off in this author's head.

The idea that two men, based on the supposed testimony of a 15 year-old girl, created a theory that took the evangelical world by storm, resolutely burying the Posttrib Rapture doctrine (which was allegedly

the one theory that was known and believed at the time). If this is true, then these two men were *more* than men. They were sorcerers or wizards, capable of bamboozling the church into believing something that according to every Posttribber did not exist before.

No other cult has ever managed to do this with any of their aberrant beliefs, yet we are to believe that these two men not only orchestrated this, but managed it, so that the PreTrib Rapture position became the *only* position that evangelical Christianity knew and believed.

This is no different from when the "Jews" are accused of being behind the attacks on the World Trade Towers. Something is wrong and it is most likely wrong in the camp of those who believe a conspiracy exists.

Chapter 6

With Vim and Vigor

With all of the Eschatology arguments being tossed about with vim and vigor, we know that for the Posttribulationist, both the Tribulation and the Rapture are far off. For the PreTribber, it is as if the Rapture will happen before the close of another day. Evangelist Paul Washer indicated that when Jesus returns, we will *then* understand Revelation perfectly. This is his way of saying that we should *not* dwell on Eschatology, nor should we try to puzzle through these types of mysteries of Scripture, with the Lord's help. Washer apparently believes that by doing so, we become sidetracked. Certainly, this can and does happen, with Christians going way beyond the bounds of Scripture when, for instance, they decide that God has "revealed" (another) date for when the Rapture will occur. These guesses are patently ridiculous and should stop.

However, it is not merely in areas of Eschatology where Christians have a tendency to get off on tangents. Christians can get off-track just about anywhere, turning some aspect of our relationship with Christ into a form of legalism. When that occurs, problems begin to emerge. Do you believe for instance, that the Sabbath still must be kept holy, as in the days of Israel of old? If so, do you find yourself becoming irritated at other Christians who do not believe as you believe, with respect to this day? Are you a Christian who believes it is wrong to eat meat, and so it follows that to you, all Christians who eat meat are "sinning"? Do you believe as a Christian woman, that your head must always be "covered," so you go out of your way to ensure that the top of your head never sees the light of day, when in public? A long list could be made of the way in which Christians become *legalists*, allowing God's freedom to entrap us into doing things out of a forced legalism, rather than a love for the Lord.

Eschatology is on the front burner these days because of all that is happening in the Middle East. Couple this with the fact that we have a Pro-Muslim president and there exists the makings of fireworks in that situation. In many ways, aspects of Eschatology are being fulfilled (or at least lined up), right before our eyes as never before. Things in the Middle East have progressed to a point where the world literally expects someone to set off a nuclear explosion. This is not far-fetched, or beyond the realm of possibility. It has brought the world to the edge of a nuclear holocaust.

Are we heading toward the period that Jesus described as the worst this world will ever experience? If there is any merit in understanding His words in a literal way (not literal*istic*), then the answer is 'yes.' It is too obvious to be otherwise. Do we *know* beyond doubt when these things will occur? Absolutely not. The Bible – while it gives a type of chronology for these events, it does not provide a timeline for the *start* of these events. We do know from the Olivet Discourse however, that once they begin, they will continue until all has been fulfilled.

So what is the point of all of this? It is simple. Are we living for Christ *now*? Do I consider each new day to be my *last*? Am I going through each day that the Lord gives me considering the fact that before the new day ends, I may be gone? I am *not* talking about the Rapture. I am talking about my *death*. Do you know when your death will occur? Do I? The answer is without equivocation, "no." I cannot count on the Rapture to whisk me away from this earth. It would be wonderful to experience the Rapture as Enoch did. It would be thrilling to go from this life to the next, alive, completely bypassing death. The Rapture for this generation is no guarantee. What *is* a guarantee is *death* for each person. I will likely die before the Rapture and/or Tribulation breaks out onto the world's scene, but possibly not.

In light of this fact, am I prepared to stand before the Lord knowing that I lived my life worshiping Him, dying to self in order to better serve Him, fulfilling His will for my life, and in essence, glorifying Him in all that I do, say and think? Those opposed to the PreTrib Rapture position say that PreTribbers are deceived, deluded, and even on their way to hell. I have personally been on the receiving end of those comments. They believe and feel at liberty to say these things all because of *their* erroneous thinking that causes them to believe that Pretribbers are *escapists*. We live anyway we want to live, shoving Christ as far to the back of the closet as we can, enjoying this sin, that sin, being lazy, unspiritual and immature. We hobnob with the world, join in their sin, laugh at holiness and we do that all because we believe that we will be saved from the Tribulation.

If that is true, then that particular "Christian" who thinks and lives like that can count on one thing: the fact that he is likely not an authentic Christian from the start. The condemnatory tone from those who firmly believe that PreTribbers are doomed to hell, is an attitude born of judgment, and this judgment is not only wrong, but it is based on a human straw man argument that has no basis in fact.

While there are many "tares" within the visible Church, this fact does not prove in any way, shape or form, that all who believe in a PreTrib Rapture live as the Posttribber charges. In fact, the Posttribber's assessment of the Pretribber is unrecognizable in either myself or anyone I know who believes in a PreTrib Rapture position. It is a handy, self-aggrandizing, pride-producing, and false assessment of the PreTribber. However, the Posttribber has built their case against the PreTribber and it remains.

One is forced to ask, in the midst of all the spiteful rhetoric and hate-filled verbiage, *who is anyone to judge?* Moreover, have the people opposed to the PreTrib Rapture position considered the fact that *they* may die long before the Tribulation begins? So intent are they to want to go through the Tribulation, in order to somehow prove to the Lord that they are "worthy," it seems obvious that many will actually be disappointed when the Lord calls them home before the Tribulation starts.

The reality for the Christian is that we are guaranteed a meeting with death, as we move from this life to the next. If we are part of that fortunate group which is raptured off the planet to be instantly with the Lord, then that is wonderful. If not, *still* wonderful. In either case, the end of our journey whether through death or rapture is the same: immediately being in the presence of the Lord, and when we see Him, we will be like Him. All who realize this purify themselves (cf. 1 John 3:2).

In the meantime, stop calling me a heretic, and many other things, just because *you* believe that I am wrong about the Rapture. I am not sitting on my easy chair, eating chips and salsa, doing nothing until that moment when the Rapture occurs. I am a Christian, loving and serving my Lord on a daily basis, albeit imperfectly. I do not hold out the hope of the Rapture "saving" me from this planet. I hold out the hope of death ushering me into His presence. If I am wrong about the Rapture and I wind up living through the Tribulation, then there is more of an opportunity to glorify Him and His Name through the experiences of my life, during that time. In any case, does it matter?

We need to dispense with the straw man arguments, which serve to condemn, based on nothing but man's imperfect thinking, and we need to get back to the Word and the Word only. For too long, those opposed to the PreTrib Rapture have moved into the extra-biblical for their "proof," however unfortunately their "proof" has largely come up sadly lacking. It has only convinced those who already believed it and it has done *nothing* to open the door to actual dialogue and discussion.

Too many Posttribbers today are judgmental, unkind, uncharitable, and filled with pride. They take their cue from their leader; Dave MacPherson; a man who is said to be living in "survivalist" mode in an earthen home in Utah, waiting for the Tribulation to begin. They have no right to judge and no right to condemn, yet they continue doing so.

Please do me a huge favor, and stop condemning me because I am "stupid" enough to see PreTrib Rapture position in the Bible. Far from living *for* myself, it has given me *great* impetus to live for Him in greater measure, *because* I could be called home at any moment, whether by my natural death or through Rapture. In either case, I will not live forever and while I do not know the day or the hour of the Rapture OR my death, it is much more probable that my death will occur long before the Rapture does. And guess what? I am *ready* for it! Are you?

Chapter 7

Always Ready and Waiting?

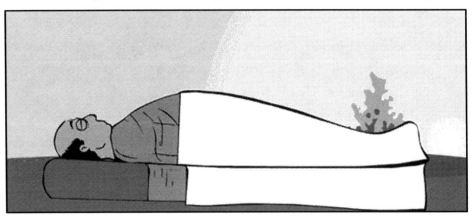

In the parable of the servants found in Luke 12:35-48, we see a scenario in which some of the servants got lazy, began to beat the other servants, and essentially stopped watching for the Master's return. The fact that they stopped watching, which in effect means they stopped expecting the Lord of the household to return at any moment, gave way to laziness and ill treatment of the others.

A great deal has been read into this parable, including the fact that the Master of the house is said to have gone to a wedding celebration. The truth of the parable lies within the pattern of the slaves. Note that some of the slaves stopped to think about the situation, and then said, "*My master is delayed in returning.*" It was because of this thinking that these slaves began "*to beat the other slaves, both men and women, and to eat, drink, and get drunk.*" What is the point here? Doubting the return of the master of the house created problems. We see this today with Preterists, and others, who teach that the Lord returned spiritually in A.D. 70, when the Romans destroyed Jerusalem and the Temple. If you pick up reading material written by some of these individuals, you read some of the most antagonistic, sarcastic ridicule of those who believe in a literal return of Christ that ever exists in written form. Some of these individuals know no bounds of good taste, and certainly do not understand how to approach a subject graciously.

The entire tone and portent of the parable states unequivocally that we should always be ready for the Lord's return. We should always be living with an attitude of expectancy. In fact, the parable makes it clear that the Master of the house could have returned at any moment. The parable loses its impact immediately if the directive given by the master of the house before he left that he could return at any moment, was not true. Think about it for a moment. The master of the house goes to a wedding. As he leaves, he says, "Not sure when I'll be back, but expect me to return at any moment." He leaves, but the slaves know perfectly well that it would take him three weeks travel time to get to the wedding celebration, then another three weeks to get back from it. In the meantime, their master had not given any indication that he was going to return directly from the wedding itself.

By this point, the slaves know that they have at least six weeks of lead-time, so they wait for six weeks. Six weeks goes by, and then more time continues. They are now at a point of heightened alert, so they make sure things are in order, they do their daily chores and ensure that all of the master's household business is performed, as if he was actually there.

More time goes by, and still the master of the house does not return. Some of them begin to believe that he became sidetracked. In fact, as more time goes by, the greater the chance of the master returning at any moment, yet some of the slaves begin to think that he is never returning. Maybe he has been hurt, or even killed? Maybe something took hold of him so thoroughly that he has no interest in his house anymore.

In other words, the parable is clear that the longer the master is away, the more reason there is for people to doubt that he will ever return, in spite of the fact that the longer he is away, the greater the chances of his imminent (or any moment) return. It is obvious that most of the slaves continued to work and do their expected chores, dutifully working for the master, as if he was actually present with them. A few of them became convinced that he was not going to return at all, and began to trifle with the well-being of the other slaves. They likely started to put the word out that the master of the house was not intending to return at all, or like our Preterists today, turned Christ's physical return into a "spiritual" return. He is still going to return, but no eye will see Him.

Please note that the parable also indicates that *nothing* is to occur prior to the master's return. He will simply appear. One moment he is not there and the next, he is there. There is nothing in the parable, which would give notification of his impending return. He simply returns and when he does, he sees that some of his servants have been and are mistreating the others. He would quickly put a stop to that and mete out punishment.

As indicated, a lot has been read out of this parable, from the timing of the wedding celebration that the master of the house attends, to everything else. With parables, it is best to go from the largest to the smallest. In other words, the overriding message of this particular parable (like most parables), is not found in the minutiae. It is found in the theme, which runs through it and the theme is being prepared for the return of the master of the house. We see if in verse 46 of Luke 12, *"then the master of that slave will come on a day when he does not expect him and at an hour he does not foresee, and will cut him in two, and assign him a place with the unfaithful."*

Notice the servant knew the Lord's will (v. 48), which was that he was supposed to continue to watch, fully prepared for the fact that the Lord of the house could arrive at any point in time. Christ is *not* speaking in generalities here. He is not saying, "Look, I'm telling you that you should always be alert for my return, even though the Tribulation is going to occur first and after seven years, *then* I'll be back." If that is the case, the parable loses its impact.

When Christ spoke this parable, He was speaking to the house of Israel, who would live through the Tribulation (and the Remnant also). Then they would come to the point of realizing that Christ was on the verge of returning. However, there is an obvious message here for the Church as well and that message is that the Rapture could occur at any moment. Since the Rapture could happen at any moment, it behooves us to be prepared for its occurrence at any time.

Think about how quickly we as human beings lose interest in things. Imagine if a parent said to a child, "Jimmy, be ready to go to Disneyland. It could happen any day now that we will all jump in the car, head to Anaheim and play for a couple of days at Disneyland." So little Jimmy starts thinking about all the fun he will have at Disneyland. Each day he wakes up, he rises to a new day of expectation, a day when he may find himself heading to Disneyland. If the parents were being literal, then we can expect them to mean that any day now, they could all pile into the car, and drive toward Disneyland.

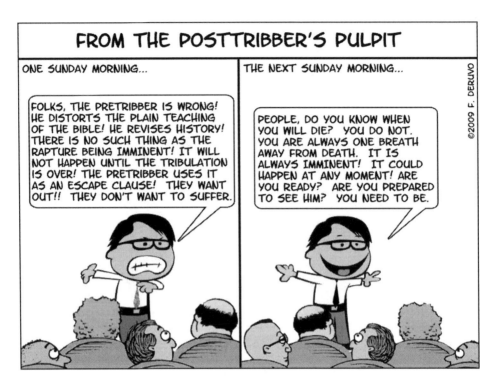

Here is a similar situation. Mom says to Janie, "Janie, be ready because when your father comes home, we will be heading to Disneyland any day after that." While little Janie is excited, she also knows that they are not going to head to Disneyland until something very important happens; the return of her father from Iraq, where he is stationed. She knows that he is not coming home for another six months at least – could even be longer, or possibly shorter - so while she is excited about Disneyland, the reality of the situation tempers her enthusiasm. Certainly, she knows that going to Disneyland cannot occur until her father returns and that will not happen for at least another six months.

Now, there is little point to this parable if in fact, the Lord's return was not imminent. If we know that He will not return until after the Tribulation (not stepping out of the 3rd heaven to Rapture His Bride at some indeterminate point before His physical, 2nd Coming), then there is absolutely no point or reason to watch for His return. None. Zilch.

Zippo. Nada. We would have at attitude of waiting only to be continually frustrated. It would be like waiting for father of the house to walk in at any moment yet the father is clearly in Iraq fighting a war, and will not be home for at least another 6 to 12 months.

This particular parable in Luke clearly speaks of imminency – a point in which the master of the house could return at any moment. If the master cannot actually return until certain events have taken place, then the immediacy and imminency of the situation changes drastically. We know that certain events are transpiring in the spiritual realm and we know that He cannot return until the fullness of the Gentiles comes in, but we do not know when the fullness of the Gentiles will be reached. That is something that, as far as we are concerned, could happen at any moment. We are not privy to the remaining number of Gentiles which must "come in" before that has been fulfilled. Is it one more? Ten more? One hundred more? A million more? Only God knows.

What we *do* know is that there is going to be a period of time on this earth, which is slated to last for seven years. Following this event, the Lord returns *physically* to the earth. Since we do not know when the Tribulation will begin, we do not know when He will return. However, when the Tribulation actually *begins*, it will be relatively easy to figure out when Jesus will return. In fact, it will be a no-brainer. The mystery is gone once the Tribulation actually begins, with the signing of the covenant with Israel and other parties of the Middle East, spearheaded by the Antichrist. It is difficult to see how Christ could have been referring to His actual Second Coming only since knowing the day is not going to be difficult at all to figure out. Could Jesus then also be referring to the Rapture of the Church, since there are no signs preceding it of which we are aware? This makes more sense, especially when compared with the concept of imminency.

We do not know when the Rapture will occur. Therefore, every day should be lived as if it was going to happen today. We should be about the Father's business with the understanding that before this day closes, we could be ushered into His presence. Does that scenario bother you? You feel as if you are not being true to the integrity of Scripture. Fine, then instead of the Rapture, substitute the phrase "your/my death." Are there any logical arguments at all that would prohibit you from believing that before this day ends, your life could also end?

It really does not matter who you are or what your particular set of beliefs are regarding the Rapture. One thing is certain. All people are going to die at some point and we will generally have no knowledge of our impending death before we die. Granted, people who have cancer or some other disease that defies medicine's ability to heal it, do have some idea how much more time they have until their death. Most of us do not. Most of us live life, go to work, run errands, go to school, and do a million things that everyone does, with little to no thought of our imminent death. When we jump in the car for a quick trip to the gas station or the grocery store, we do not stop to think that we may not be returning to our home and family. This is not to say that we should become paranoid about life, never wanting to leave our home. We should rest in the knowledge that the Lord is in control of our life and destiny.

Understanding that our death is always imminent should create within us a respect for the time that we *do* have, so that we make the most of that time, appreciating life, and letting go of the things that do not matter. We should also understand that the time we have remaining is extremely valuable, and we are accountable for it. Did you witness to anyone today? Did you spend time in prayer today? Did you get to know the Lord through His Word a bit more today? Did you see more of Christ developed in you today?

Posttribbers can complain as loudly as they want to about their belief that the PreTrib Rapture is nonsense. Good. Go for it. That is fine. If Posttribbers do not want to understand imminency in terms of at any moment, with respect to the Rapture, that is fine. However, do not make the mistake of doing that where your death is concerned, because your death is *always* imminent. You cannot argue that away. You cannot say that the imminency of your death is based on a conspiracy of a 15 year-old girl, carried forward first by J. N. Darby, then C. I. Scofield. You have no one to castigate or rake over the coals. You have no one to accuse of revisionism.

Death will take all of us and the people who are stupid enough to believe that they will live until the ripe old age of (fill in the blank), are unfortunately just that: stupid. They have not only mishandled God's Word in that respect, but they have provided themselves with excuse after excuse to live the way they want to because they believe they have "plenty of time" to do what they need to do.

So, dear Posttribber and others who believe that the Pretribber is deluded, deceived, heretical and on the path to hell because we understand the Scriptures to teach a PreTrib Rapture, what is it *you* have to say for yourself with respect to *death*? As indicated earlier, death *trumps* the Rapture. My death will likely occur before the Rapture or the Tribulation, but only God knows with certainty. The only thing I am counting on is that one day I will die and on that day, I will see Jesus, my Savior, and my Lord. In the meantime, because I know that my death is a matter of fact, it prompts me to live my life the only biblical way there is to live: putting Christ first, serving Him with gladness, and looking forward to seeing His wonderful face.

Go ahead; continue to argue that the Rapture is not happening BEFORE the Tribulation. Argue that it is going to occur at the same time as the Second Coming, *after* the Tribulation. Tell me that I am deluded, deceived, and dead in sin, hell bound because I believe in the PreTrib Rapture. Say that those who believe in the PreTrib Rapture become unspiritual, carnal, filled with sin, and more. However, you are going to have to think fast to come up with the reason why the very same arguments do *not* work for understanding that the Scriptures teach that each person's death is *always* imminent. Should not this also make me just as deluded, just as deceived and just as hell bound?

Following through logically with the idea that believing the Rapture will provide me with the escape clause needed for the coming Tribulation, which apparently causes me to live carnally, unspiritually, enjoying sin-filled living, and dragging Christ's Name through the mud, the exact same *must* be said regarding my belief that I could die at any moment. There is *no* difference.

If you cannot provide me with the same reasonings why believing that my death might occur at any moment, without warning, causing me to live carnally, then you've got some serious explaining to do about why the PreTrib Rapture *does* cause deception and delusion, while the imminency of my death does *not*.

Take your time. Seriously consider your response. I will wait...

Resources for Your Library:

BOOKS & DVDs:

- The Antichrist and His Kingdom, by Thomas Ice
- Basis of the Premillennial Faith, The, by Charles C. Ryrie
- Biblical Hermeneutics, by Milton S. Terry
- The Case for Zionism, by Thomas Ice
- Charting the End Times, by LaHaye and Ice
- Christian and Social Responsibility, The, by Charles C. Ryrie
- Church in Prophecy, The by John F. Walvoord
- The Coming Cashless Society, by Thomas Ice and Timothy J Demy
- Dictionary of Premillennial Theology, Mal Couch, Editor
- Dispensationalism Tomorrow & Beyond, by Christopher Cone, Editor
- Exploring the Future, by John Phillips
- Footsteps of the Messiah, by Arnold G. Fruchtenbaum
- Future Israel (Why Christian Anti-Judaism Must Be Challenged), by E. Ray Clendenen, Ed.
- The Great Tribulation, Debate with DeMar and Ice (DVD)
- Interpreting the Bible, by A. Berkeley Mickelsen
- Israelology, by Arnold G. Fruchtenbaum
- Moody Handbook of Theology, The by Paul Enns
- Mountains of Israel, The, by Norma Archbold
- Pre-Wrath Rapture Answered, The, by Lee W. Brainard
- Prolegomena, by Christopher Cone
- Promises of God, The, a Bible Survey, by Christopher Cone
- There Really Is a Difference! by Renald Showers
- Things to Come, by J. Dwight Pentecost
- The Truth Behind Left Behind, by Thomas Ice and Mark Hitchcock
- Truth War, The, by John MacArthur
- What on Earth is God Doing? By Renald Showers

Resources for Your Library (cont'd)

INTERNET:

- Ariel Ministries — www.ariel.org
- Bible Prophecy Today — bible-prophecy-today.blogspot.com/
- Friends of Israel — www.foi.org
- Grace to You — www.gty.org
- Grant Jeffrey Ministries — www.grantjeffrey.com/
- Koinonia House — www.khouse.org/
- PreTrib Rapture Research — www.pre-trib.org/
- Prophecy Central — www.bible-prophecy.com/
- Prophecy in the News — www.prophecyinthenews.com/
- Prophecy Today — www.prophecytoday.com/
- Rapture Ready — www.raptureme.com/
- Rapture Research Website — www.pretribulationrapture.com/
- Rightly Dividing — www.righly-dividing.com
- Study-Grow-Know — www.studygrowknow.com
- Thomas Ice Writings — www.raptureme.com/ttcol.html
- Tyndale Theological Seminary — www.tyndale.edu

Made in the USA
Charleston, SC
19 January 2010